Cardigans
ESSENTIAL
KNITS

ten hand knit
cardigan designs

quail studio

quail studio

Published in 2016 by
Quail Publishing
The Old Forge
Market Square
Toddington
Bedfordshire, LU5 6BP
UK

ISBN: 978-0-9927707-5-4

Conceived, designed and produced by

quail studio

Art Editor: Georgina Brant
Graphic Design: Quail Studio
Technical Editor: Emma Osmond
Pattern Checking: Jacky Edwards
Photography: Jesse Wild
Creative Director: Darren Brant
Yarn Support: Rowan Yarns
Designer: Quail Studio
Model: Hollie ~ BMA Models

Printed in the UK

British Library Cataloguing in Publication Data
A catalogue record for this book is available from the British Library

@quail_studio

contents

introduction

The second in the series of ESSENTIAL knits from quail studio comes the Cardigan collection. Designed to be an appealing collection where each design is wearable, and can be styled in different ways – completing your essential wardrobe.

The quail studio team have taken simple shapes, paired with a minimalist colour palette and simple styling to bring to life the exquisite yarn from Rowan.

Featuring a core collection of hand knit cardigans, with various different fits and styles. So if you are after a more relaxed chunky cardigan or lighter weight, more fitted look - Essential Cardigans has it all.

Hand knit your own stylish essential knitted wardrobe, we just know you will not be disappointed!

quail studio team
xoxo

BINKY
*rowan brushed
fleece*

WHITNEY
rowan superfine
4ply

CHLOE
*rowan creative
linen*

EMMA
rowan big wool

KENDALL
rowan handknit cotton

LO
*rowan pure wool
superwash worsted*

GIGI
rowan cocoon

OLIVIA
rowan baby merino silk dk

KIRSTY
*rowan brushed
fleece*

ELLIE
*rowan summerlite
4ply*

Binky

SIZES: XS (S, M, L, XL, XXL)

YARN: 6 (6, 7, 7, 8, 8) balls of Rowan Brushed Fleece (shown in shade 263)

NEEDLES: 5mm and 6mm (8US and 10US)

EXTRAS: Stitch holder

TENSION: 13sts and 19rows = 10cm measured over st st using 6mm needles.

BACK:
Using 5mm needles, cast on 60(62,66,70,74,78)sts and starting with a K row, work in g st for 4cm, ending with a WS row.

Change to 6mm needles and starting with a K row, work in st st until work measures 32(33,34,35,35,35)cm, ending with a WS row.

SHAPE ARMHOLES:
Cast off 3sts at beg of next 2 rows. 54[56, 60, 64, 68, 72]sts.

Dec 1 st at each end of 5 foll alt rows. 44[46, 50, 54, 58, 62]sts

Cont straight until armhole measures 23(23,23,23,24,25)cm, ending with a WS row.

SHAPE BACK NECK:
Patt 12(13,15,17,19,21)sts, turn.
Work 1 row.
Cast off.

Slip centre 20sts onto a stitch holder and work other side to match.

LEFT FRONT:

Using 5mm needles, cast on 30(31,33,35,37,39)sts and starting with a K row, work in g st for 4cm, ending with a WS row.

Change to 6mm needles and starting with a K row, work in st st until work measures 32(33,34,35,35,35)cm, ending with a WS row.

SHAPE ARMHOLE:

Cast off 3sts at beg of next row, work to end. 27[28, 30, 32, 34, 36]sts.

Dec 1 st at the beg of 5 foll alt rows. 22[23, 25, 27, 29, 31]sts.

Cont straight until armhole measures 23(23,23,23,24,25)cm, ending with a RS row.

SHAPE NECK:

Next row (WS): Cast off 8sts, work to end. 14[15, 17, 19, 21, 23]sts.

Decrease 1 st at neck edge on next 2 rows. 12[13, 15, 17, 19, 21]sts.

Cont until front matches back.
Cast off.

RIGHT FRONT: Work as left front, reversing all shapings.

SLEEVES (make two):

Using 5mm needles, cast on 30(30, 32,32,34,36)sts and starting with a K row, work in g st for 4cm.

Change to 6mm needles and starting with a K row, work in st st, increasing 1 st at each end of 5th row and every foll 4th row until 60(60,62,62,64,66)sts.

Cont straight until work measures 43(43,44,44,45,46)cm ending with a WS row.

SHAPE SLEEVE TOP:

Cast off 3sts at beg of next 2 rows. 54[54, 56, 56, 58, 60]sts.

Dec 1 st at each end of next 3 foll alt rows. 48[48, 50, 50, 52, 54]sts.

Dec 1 st at each end of next 3 rows. 42[42, 44, 44, 46, 48]sts.

Work 1 row.

Cast off.

FINISHING:

Join shoulder seams.

FRONT AND NECK BANDS:

LEFT FRONT: Using a 6mm needles, with RS facing and starting at the top of left front edge, pick up and knit 69(69,70,71,72,73)sts down left front edge.
Knit 1 row.
Cast off loosely.

RIGHT FRONT:
Work as for left front, starting at the base of the right front edge.

NECK:
Using 6mm needles, with RS facing and starting at top of the right front band, pick up and knit 19sts along right side of neck, 20sts from stitch holder at back neck and19sts down left neck shaping. (58sts)

Knit 1 row.

Cast off loosely.

Sew in sleeves.

Join side and sleeve seams.

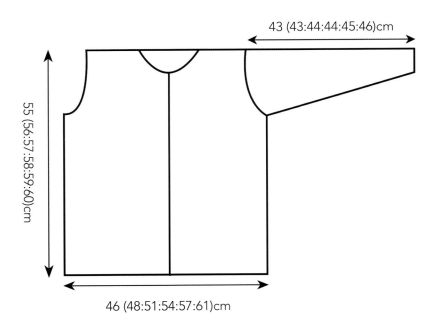

43 (43:44:44:45:46)cm

55 (56:57:58:59:60)cm

46 (48:51:54:57:61)cm

Whitney

SIZES: XS (S, M, L, XL, XXL)

YARN: 10 (10, 11, 11, 12, 13) balls of Rowan Super Fine Merino 4ply (shown in shade 269)

NEEDLES: 2.75mm (2US) and 3mm (3US)

EXTRAS: Stitch holder

TENSION: 28sts and 36rows = 10cm measured over st st using 3mm needles.

BACK:
Using 2.75mm needles, cast on 136 (142, 148, 154, 160, 166) sts and work 4cm in moss st ending with a WS row.

Change to 3mm needles and starting with a K row cont in st st until work measures 47(47, 48, 48, 48, 48)cm, ending with a WS row.

SHAPE ARMHOLES:
Cast off 3(3,4,4,5,5)sts at beg of next 2 rows. 130[136, 140, 146, 150, 156]sts.

Dec 1 st at each end of every alt 3 (3,3,4,4,5) rows. 124[130, 134, 138, 142, 146]sts.

Cont straight until armhole measures 20(21,21,22,23,24)cm, ending with a WS row.

SHAPE BACK NECK:
Patt 37(40,42,44,46,48)sts turn.

P2tog, work to end. 36[39, 41, 43, 45, 47]sts.

Cast off.

Slip centre 50sts onto a holder and work other side to match.

LEFT FRONT:

Using 2.75mm needles, cast on 117(120, 123,126,129,132)sts and work 4cm in moss st, ending with a WS row.

Change to 3mm needles and starting with a K row, cont in st st until work measures 47(47, 48, 48, 48, 48)cm, ending with a WS row.

SHAPE ARMHOLES:

Cast off 3(3,4,4,5,5)sts at beg of next row, work to end. 114[117, 119, 122, 124, 127]sts.

Dec 1 st at beg of every alt 3 (3,3,4,4,5) rows. 111[114, 116, 118, 120, 122]sts.

Cont straight until armhole measures 20(21,21,22,23,24)cm, ending with a WS row.

SHAPE NECK:

K36(39,41,43,45,47)sts, turn and leave rem sts on a stitch holder.

Next row: Purl
Starting with a K row, work 4 rows in st st.
Cast off.
Rejoin yarn to rem sts, work 1 row.
Cast off.

RIGHT FRONT:

Work as left front, reversing all shapings.

SLEEVES (make two):

Using 2.75mm needles, cast on 58(58,58,62,64,66)sts and work in moss st for 4cm, ending with a WS row.

Change to 3mm needles and starting with a K row, work in st st, increasing 1 st at each end of the 5th and every foll 4th row until 116(116,116, 120,120, 124)sts.

Cont straight until work measures 47(48,48,49,50,51)cm, ending with a WS row.

SHAPE SLEEVE TOP:

Cast off 3sts at beg of next 2 rows. 110[110, 110, 114, 114, 118]sts.

Dec 1 st at each end of every alt 3 (3,3,4,4,5) rows. 104[104, 104, 106, 106, 108]sts.

Work 1 row.

Cast off.

FINISHING:

Join shoulder seams.

Using 2.75mm needles with right side facing pick up and knit 5sts at the front neck of right front, 4sts at back of neck, 50sts from stitch holder at back neck, 4sts up side of back neck to shoulder, 5sts along front neck of left front. (68)sts.

Knit 3 rows.
Cast off.

Stitch edge of pick up sts to front edge.

Sew in sleeves.
Join side and sleeve seams.

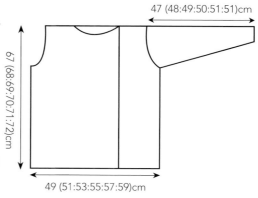

47 (48:49:50:51:51)cm

67 (68:69:70:71:72)cm

49 (51:53:55:57:59)cm

Chloe

SIZES: XS (S, M, L, XL, XXL)

YARN USAGE: 7 (8, 8, 9, 9, 10) balls of Rowan Creative Linen (shown in shade 621)

NEEDLES: 4mm and 4.5mm (6US and 7US)

TENSION: 18sts and 24rows = 10cm measured over double moss st using 4.5mm needles.

EXTRAS: 6 x medium sized buttons, Cable needle

MOSS STITCH:
Row 1: Knit 1, purl 1
Row 2: Purl 1, knit 1

BACK: Using 4mm needles, cast on 116(120,124,128,132,136)sts and work 6cm in moss st, ending with a RS row.
Next row : *Work 18(20, 22, 24, 26, 28)sts, M1, work 3sts, M1, work 3sts, M1, rep from * twice more, work to end.
125(129, 133, 137, 141, 145)sts

Change to 4.5mm needles and cont as follows:

Beg and ending rows as indicated on the chart for the back and repeating the 8 row patt throughout, cont until work measures 70(71, 72, 72, 73, 73)cm ending with a WS row.

SHAPE BACK NECK:
Patt 45(47, 49, 51, 53, 55)sts turn.

Work back across stitches as set.

Cast off.

Slip centre 35sts onto a stitch holder and work other side to match.

LEFT FRONT:
Using 4mm needles, cast on 52(54, 56, 58, 60, 62)sts and work 6cm in moss st, ending with a RS row.

Next row: *Work 18(20, 22, 24, 26, 28) sts, M1, work 3sts, M1, work 3sts, M1, patt to end. 55[57, 59, 61, 63, 65]sts

Change to 4.5mm needles and cont as follows:

Beg and ending rows as indicated on the chart for the left front and repeating the 8 row patt throughout, cont until work measures 60(61, 62, 62, 63, 63)cm ending after a RS row.

SHAPE NECK:
Cast off 6sts and pattern to end. 49[51, 53, 55, 57, 59]sts.

Next row: Patt to last 2 sts, work 2 sts tog. 48[50, 52, 54, 56, 58]sts.

Continue to decrease one st at neck edge on every row until 45(47, 49, 51, 53, 55)sts remain.

Cont until work matches length of back

Cast off.

RIGHT FRONT: Work as left front, using right front chart and reversing all shapings.

SLEEVES (make two):
Using 4mm needles, cast on 48(50, 52, 54, 56, 58)sts and work 6cm in moss st, ending with a WS row.

Change to 4.5mm needles and cont as follows:

Beg and ending rows as indicated on

the chart for the sleeve and repeating the 53 row patt throughout, increase 1 stitch at each

end of 5th and every following 4th row until 88(90, 92, 94, 96, 98)sts.

Cont straight until work measures 39(40, 41, 42, 43, 44)cm, ending with a WS row.

Cast off.

FINISHING:
Join shoulder seams.

LEFT FRONT EDGE:
Using 4mm needles and with RS facing, starting at top of left front edge, pick up and knit 96(98, 100, 102, 104, 106)sts evenly down front edge. Working in moss st as folls.
Next Row: (K1, P1) to end
Foll row: (P1,K1) to end
Rep these 2 rows 4 times more.
Cast off.

RIGHT FRONT EDGE:
Using 4mm needles and with RS facing, starting at bottom edge of right front edge, pick up and knit 96(98, 100, 102, 104, 106)sts evenly up front edge. Working in moss st as folls.
Next Row: (K1, P1) to end
Foll row: (P1,K1) to end
Rep these 2 rows 2 times more and first row once more.
Cast off.

Buttonhole row: Moss st 4(5,6,6,6,6) sts, patt2tog, yfwd * moss st 15(15,15,15,16,16)sts, patt2tog, yfwd, rep from * to last 4(5,6,6,6,6)sts, patt2tog, yfwd, moss st to end.
Work 4 rows in moss st patt.
Cast off.

COLLAR:
Using 4mm needles and with RS facing,
starting at top of the right front band,
pick up and knit, 35sts along right front
edge of neck, 2sts across to shoulder,
35sts from stitch holder, 2sts across to
shoulder, and 34sts along left front edge
of neck. (108sts)

Next row: (K2, P2) to end.

Rep last row until work measures 12cm.

Cast off.

Sew in sleeves.
Join side and sleeve seams.

Attach buttons.

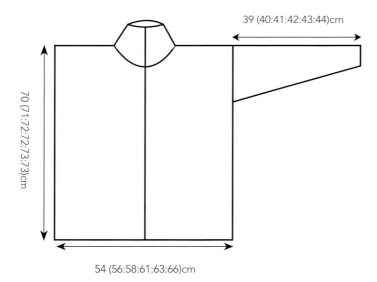

39 (40:41:42:43:44)cm

70 (71:72:72:73:73)cm

54 (56:58:61:63:66)cm

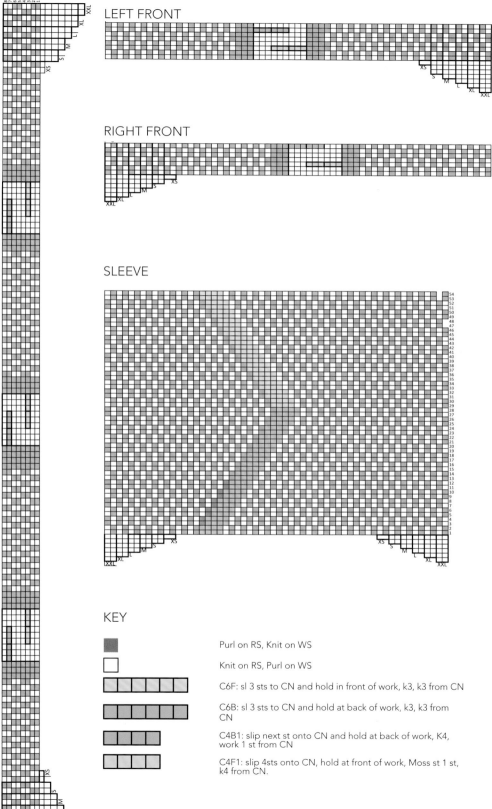

LEFT FRONT

RIGHT FRONT

SLEEVE

BACK

KEY

▓	Purl on RS, Knit on WS
□	Knit on RS, Purl on WS
	C6F: sl 3 sts to CN and hold in front of work, k3, k3 from CN
	C6B: sl 3 sts to CN and hold at back of work, k3, k3 from CN
	C4B1: slip next st onto CN and hold at back of work, K4, work 1 st from CN
	C4F1: slip 4sts onto CN, hold at front of work, Moss st 1 st, k4 from CN.

Emma

SIZES: S/M (M/L, L/XL)

YARN USAGE: 8 (9, 10) balls of Rowan Big Wool (shown in shade 064)

NEEDLES: 10mm (15US)

EXTRAS: Stitch holder

TENSION: 10sts and 12rows = 10cm measured over st st using 10mm needles.

BACK:
Using 10mm needles, cast on 60(68,76)sts.
Row 1: (K1, P1) to end,
Rep last row three time more.
Now work in basket weave st as folls:
Row 1: (RS) Knit.
Row 2: (P4,K4) rep to last 4 sts, P4.
Row 3: (K4, P4) rep to last 4 sts, K4.
Row 4: As row 2.

Row 5: Knit.
Row 6: (K4,P4) rep to last 4sts, K4.
Row 7: (P4,K4) rep to last 4sts, P4.
Row 8: As row 6.
Row 9: Knit.
Rep from row 2 to 9 throughout.

Cont as set until work measures 67(68,69)cm, ending with a WS row.

SHAPE BACK NECK:
Patt 20(24, 28)sts, turn.
Patt 1 row.
Cast off.
Slip centre 20sts onto a stitch holder and work other side to match.

LEFT FRONT:
Using 10mm needles, cast on
40(44,48)sts and work rib as set for
back for 4 rows.
Now work as folls:
Row 1: (RS) Knit.
Row 2: P24(28,32), (P4,K4) rep
to end.
Row 3: (P4,K4) rep twice, Knit
24(28,32).
Row 4: As row 2.
Row 5: Knit.
Row 6: P24(28,32), (K4,P4) rep
to end.
Row 7: (K4,P4) rep twice, K24(28,32).
Row 8: As row 6.
Row 9: Knit.
Rep from row 2 to 9 throughout until
work measures 67(68, 69)cm ending
with a WS row.

SHAPE NECK:
Cast off 20(24,28)sts and starting with
a K row, cont to work on rem 20sts in
st st for a further 11cm.
Cast off.

RIGHT FRONT:
Work as left front, reversing all shapings.

SLEEVES (make two):
Using 10mm needles, cast on
21(21,25)sts.
Next row: (K1, P1) to last st, K1.
Inc 1 st at each end of 11th and foll
8th row. 25[25,29]sts.
Cont in rib patt until sleeve
measures 20cm ending with a
WS row.

Now work in basket weave st as for
back and AT THE SAME TIME, inc 1
st at each end of every alt row until
53(53,57)sts, incorporating increased
stitches into pattern.
Work straight until sleeve measures
43(43,44)cm.
Cast off.

FINISHING:
It is important to block all pieces to
the measurements of the pattern
before completing the seams.

Using 10mm, pick up 20sts from stitch
holder at back neck and starting with
a K row, work 11cm in st st.
Cast off.

Join shoulder seams.

Join back and side neck
pieces together.

Sew in sleeves and join side and
sleeve seams.

Take top corner of each front and fold
back on themselves to the inside and
slip stitch into place along neck and
part of shoulder seam.

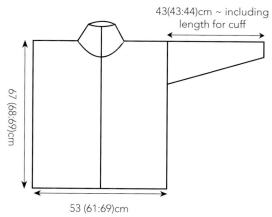

43(43:44)cm ~ including
length for cuff

67 (68:69)cm

53 (61:69)cm

Kendall

SIZES: XS (S, M, L, XL, XXL)

YARN USAGE: 17 (17, 18, 18, 19, 20) balls of Rowan Handknit Cotton (shown in shade 263)

NEEDLES: 3.25mm (3US) and 4mm (6US)

EXTRAS: Stitch holder

TENSION: 24sts and 36 rows = 10cm measured over rib pattern using 4mm needles.

RIB PATTERN:
Row 1: (RS) K3,* yfwd, Sl1 purlwise, yarn back, K3; rep from * to end
Row 2: K1,* yfwd, Sl1 purlwise, yarn back, K3; rep from * to last 2 sts, yfwd, Sl1 purlwise, yarn back ,K1.
Rep rows 1 and 2 throughout.

BACK:
Using 4mm needles, cast on 135(139,143,147,151,155)sts and work in rib pattern throughout until work measures 69(70,71,72,73,74)cm ending with a WS row.

SHAPE BACK NECK:
Patt 47(49,51,53,55,57)sts, turn.
Work 2sts tog, work to end.
46[48,50,52,54,56]sts.
Cast off.
Slip centre 41sts onto a stitch holder and work other side to match.
Cast off.

LEFT FRONT:
Using 4mm needles, cast on 63(67,71,75,79,83)sts and work in rib pattern throughout until work measures 41(42,43,44,45,46)cm, ending with a RS row.

SHAPE NECK:
Dec 1 st at neck edge on next and every following 4th row to 46(48, 50, 52, 54, 56)sts. Cont straight until work matches back, ending with a WS row. Cast off.

RIGHT FRONT:
Work as left front, reversing all shapings.

SLEEVES (make two):
Using 4mm needles, cast on 51(55,55,59,59,63)sts and work in rib pattern throughout.

Inc 1 st at each end of the 5th and every foll 4th row until 107(111,111,115,115,119)sts.

Cont straight until work measures 39(40,41,42,43,44)cm, ending with a WS row.

Cast off.

FINISHING:
Join both shoulder seams.

Using 3.25mm needles and with right side facing, starting at lower edge of right front, pick up and knit 75(77,79,81,83,85)sts along edge to beginning of V shaping, 54sts to shoulder seam, 41sts from stitch holder at back neck, 54sts down left front neck shaping and 75(77,79,81,83,85)sts down left front edge. 299[303, 307, 311, 315, 319]sts.
Next row: Purl.
Next row: Knit.
Next row: Purl.
Cast off using a 4mm needle.

Sew in sleeves.
Join side and sleeve seams.

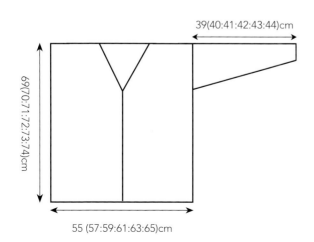

39(40:41:42:43:44)cm

69(70:71:72:73:74)cm

55 (57:59:61:63:65)cm

SIZES: XS (S, M, L, XL, XXL)

YARN USAGE: 8 (8, 9, 9, 10, 10) balls of Rowan Pure Wool Superwash Worsted (shown in shade 103)

NEEDLES: 4mm (6US) and 5mm (8US)

EXTRAS: Stitch holder, markers

TENSION: 18sts and 26 rows = 10cm measured over pattern using 5mm needles.

RIB PATTERN:
Row 1: (RS) K2, P1 rep to last 2 sts, K2.
Row 2: P2,(K1,P2) to end.

BROKEN MOSS ST:
Row 1: K1,P1 to end.
Row 2: Purl to end.
Row 3: P1,K1 to end.
Row 4: Purl to end.

BACK:
Using 4mm needles, cast on 98(104, 110, 116, 122, 128)sts and work in rib pattern until work measures 8cm ending with a WS row.

Change to 5mm needles and work in broken moss st until work measures 13cm, ending with a WS row.

Inc 1 st at each end of next row. 100[106, 112, 118, 124, 130]sts.

Cont working in broken moss st, inc 1 st at each end of every foll 14th row until 114(118, 122, 126, 130, 134)sts.

Cont straight until work measures 52(53, 54, 55, 56, 56)cms ending with a WS row.

Next row: Cast on 28(28, 28, 30, 32, 34) sts, patt to end. 142[146, 150, 156, 162, 168]sts.

Next row: Cast on 28(28, 28, 30, 32, 34)sts, patt across all sts.
170[174, 178, 186, 194, 202]sts.

Place marker at end of last row. Cont straight until work measures 25cm from marker ending with a WS row.

SHAPE BACK NECK:
Patt 67(69, 71, 75, 79, 83)sts, turn.
Work 2sts tog, work to end. 66[68, 70, 74, 78, 82]sts.
Cast off.
Slip centre 36sts onto a stitch holder and work other side to match.
Cast off.

LEFT FRONT:
Using 4mm needles, cast on 38(44, 50, 56, 62, 68)sts and work in rib pattern, until work measures 8cm ending with a WS row.

Change to 5mm needles and work in broken moss st until work measures 13cm, ending with a WS row.

Inc 1 st at side edge of next row.
39[45, 51, 57, 63, 69]sts.

Cont working in broken moss st and inc 1 st at side edge of every foll 14th row until 46(51, 56, 61, 66, 71) sts.

Cont straight until work measures 52(53, 54, 55, 56, 56)cm, ending with a WS row.

Next row: Cast on 28(28, 28, 30, 32, 34)sts, work to end. 74[79, 84, 91, 98, 105]sts.

Place marker at end of last row. Cont straight until work measures 25cm from marker, ending with a WS row.
Cast off.

RIGHT FRONT:
Work as left front reversing all shapings.

FINISHING:
Join shoulder seams.

CUFFS (make 2):
With RS facing and 4mm needles, pick up and knit 96sts along lower sleeve edge.

Row 1: P2,K1 to end.
Work in rib as set, until work measures 5cms.
Cast off in rib.

RIGHT FRONT BAND:

With RS facing and 4mm needles, pick up and knit 189(192, 195, 198, 201, 204) sts evenly along right edge, beginning at lower edge of the right front and ending at centre of back neck.
Row 1: P2, K1 to end.
Work in rib as set until work measures 17cm.
Cast off in rib.

LEFT FRONT BAND:

With RS facing and 4mm needles, pick up and knit 189(192, 195, 198, 201, 204) sts evenly along left front edge, beginning at centre of back neck and ending at lower edge of left front.
Row 1: K1, P2 to end.
Work in rib as set, until work measures 17cm.
Cast off in rib.

Join centre back neck.

Join side and sleeve seams.

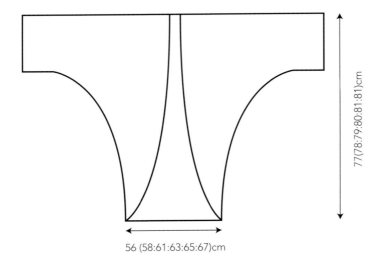

77(78:79:80:81:81)cm

56 (58:61:63:65:67)cm

Gigi

SIZES: XS (S, M, L, XL, XXL)

YARN USAGE: 7 (7, 8, 8, 9, 10) balls of Rowan Cocoon (shown in shade 836)

NEEDLES: 7mm (10 ½ US)

EXTRAS: Cable needle and stitch holder

TENSION: 14sts and 16rows = 10cm measured over st st using 7mm needles.

PATTERN NOTE: Worked in 1 piece.

LEFT FRONT EDGE CABLE:
Worked over 16sts.
Row 1: P2, K14.
Row 2: P14, K2.
Row 3: P2, K14.
Row 4: P14, K2.
Row 5: P2, C14F (slip 7sts onto CN and leave at front of work, K7, K7 from CN).
Row 6: As row 2.

Row 7: As row 1.
Row 8: As row 2.
Row 9: As row 1.
Row 10: As row 2.
Row 11: As row 1.
Row 12: As row 2.
Row 13: As row 5.
Rep from rows 6 to 13.

RIGHT FRONT EDGE CABLE:
Worked over 16sts.
Row 1: K14, P2.
Row 2: K2, P14.
Row 3: K14, P2.
Row 4: K2, P14.
Row 5: C14F (slip 7sts onto CN and leave at front of work, K7, K7 from CN), P2.
Row 6: As row 2.
Row 7: As row 1.
Row 8: As row 2.
Row 9: As row 1.

Row 10: As row 2.
Row 11: As row 1.
Row 12: As row 2.
Row 13: As row 5.
Rep from rows 6 to 13.

LEFT SLEEVE EDGE CABLE:
Worked over 10sts.
Row 1: K8, P2.
Row 2: K2, P8.
Row 3: C8F (slip 4sts onto CN and leave at front of work, K4, K4 from CN), P2.
Row 4: K2, P8.
Row 5: As row 1.
Row 6: As row 2.
Row 7: C8F (slip 4sts onto CN and leave at front of work, K4, K4 from CN), P2.
Rep from rows 4 to 7.

RIGHT SLEEVE EDGE CABLE:
Worked over 10 sts.
Row 1: P2, K8.
Row 2: P8, K2.
Row 3: P2, C8F (slip 4sts onto CN and leave at front of work, K4, K4 from CN).
Row 4: P8, K2.
Row 5: As row 1.
Row 6: As row 2.
Row 7: P2, C8F (slip 4sts onto CN and leave at front of work, K4, K4 from CN).
Rep from rows 4 to 7.

LEFT FRONT:
Using 7mm needles, cast on 42(44,46,48,50,52)sts and work 4 rows in g st.

Cont as folls:
Row 1: K24(26,28,30,32,34)sts, p2, starting at row 1, work 16sts from front edge cable pattern.
Row 2: Work 16 rows of cable pattern, K2, purl to end.
Cont to work sts as set until work measures 57(58,59,58,57,57)cm ending with a WS row.

Turn and cast on 40sts. 82[84, 86, 88, 90, 92]sts.

Starting at row 1 work 10 sts from left sleeve edge cable patt, P2, pattern to end, keeping front edge cable patt correct.

Cont working all sts as set until work measures 81(82,83,84,85,85)cm, ending with a WS row.

Put sts on a stitch holder.

RIGHT FRONT:
Work as for left front, reversing all shapings.

BACK:
Using 7mm needles, work across all sts of left front until you reach left front edge cable. Slip these 16sts onto a holder, turn and cast on 32sts for back neck. Turn back and join to right front, after slipping 16sts of right front cable edge onto a stitch holder,

then work across the remaining sts on right front. 164(168,172,176,180,184)sts

Cont working across all sts until work measures 24(24,24,26,28,28)cm from cast on stitches at back neck, ending with a WS row.

Cast off 40sts at beg of next 2 rows. 84[88,92,96,100,104]sts.

Cont straight in st st until work measures same as front to lower edge, working last 4 rows in g st.
Cast off.

LEFT FRONT EDGE:
Using 7mm needles, pick up 16sts from stitch holder at left front and continue with cable pattern until work is long enough to fit to half way across back neck. Cast off.

RIGHT FRONT EDGE:
Work as left front edge.

Join front edged together at centre of back neck.

FINISHING:
Join side and sleeve seams.

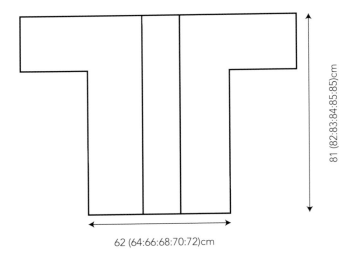

62 (64:66:68:70:72)cm

81 (82:83:84:85:85)cm

Olivia

SIZES: XS (S, M, L, XL, XXL)

YARN USAGE: 9 (9, 10, 10, 11, 11) balls of Rowan Baby Merino Silk DK (shown in shade 674)

NEEDLES: 4mm (6US), 4mm/80cm circular needle

EXTRAS: Stitch holder

TENSION: 22sts and 30rows = 10cm measured over st st using 4mm needles.

BACK:
Using 4mm needles, cast on 130(132,134,136,138,140)sts and starting wth a K row work in st st until work measures 16cm, ending with a WS row.

Inc 1 st at each end of next row and every following 6th row until 170(172,174,176,178,180)sts.

Cont straight until work measures 49(50,51,49,50,48)cm, ending with a WS row.

SHAPE SLEEVES:
Cast on 28sts at beg of next 2 rows. 226(228,230,232,234,236)sts.

Cont straight until work measures 69(70,71,72,73,74)cm, ending with a WS row.

SHAPE BACK NECK:
Patt 94(95,96,97,98,99)sts, turn.
Work back across stitches.
Cast off.
Slip centre 38sts onto a stitch holder and work other side to match.

LEFT FRONT:

Using 4mm needles, cast on 21(22,23,24,25,26)sts, and starting with a K row work 3 rows in st st, ending with a RS row.

Inc 1 st at beg of following row and then at same front edge on every foll alt 25 rows.

AT THE SAME TIME, when work measures 15cm, inc 1 st at side on following row and then every foll 6th row until 66(67,68,69,70,71) sts.

Cont straight until work measures 49(50,51,49,50,48)cm, ending with a WS row.

SHAPE SLEEVES:

Cast on 28sts at beg of next row. 94[95, 96, 97, 98, 99]sts.

Cont straight until work measures 69(70,71,72,73,74)cm, ending with a WS row.
Cast off.

RIGHT FRONT:

Work as for left front, reversing all shapings.

FINISHING:

Join shoulder seams.

SLEEVE EDGINGS (make two):

Using 4mm needles and with RS facing, pick up and knit 86(88,90,92,94,96)sts along sleeve edge.

Beg with a purl row, work 3 rows in st st.
Cast off loosely knitwise.

Join side and sleeve seams.

EDGING:

Worked in one piece. Using a circular 4mm/80cm needle, with RS facing and starting at left shoulder seam, pick up and knit 174(176,178,180,182,184) sts down left front and left lower front edge, 130(132,134,136,138,140)sts along back lower edge, 174(176,178,180,182,184)sts up right lower front and right front edge, 4sts at side of back neck, 38sts from stitch holder at back neck, and 4sts at side of back side neck.
524[530, 536, 542, 548, 554]sts

Beg with a purl row, work 3 rows in st st.

Cast off loosely knitwise.

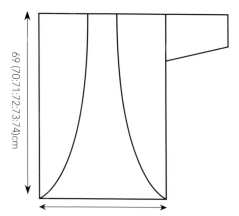

69 (70.71.72.73.74)cm

59 (60:61:62:63:64)cm

Kirsty

SIZES: XS/S (M/L: XL/XXL)

YARN USAGE: 12 (14, 16) balls of Rowan Brushed Fleece (shown in shade 262)

NEEDLES: 12mm and 15mm (17US and 19US)

EXTRAS: Stitch holders

TENSION: 7sts and 9 rows = 10cm measured over st st using 15mm needles and using yarn doubled.

NOTE: Use yarn doubled throughout.

BACK:
Using yarn doubled throughout and 12mm needles, cast on 38(46:54)sts and work 8 rows in K1, P1 rib ending with a WS row.
Change to 15mm needles and starting with a K row work in st st until work measures 100(102:104)cm, ending with a WS row.

SHAPE BACK NECK:
Patt 13(17,21)sts, turn.
Work 1 row.
Cast off.
Slip centre 12sts onto a stitch holder and work other side to match.

POCKET LININGS: (make two)
Using yarn doubled throughout and 15mm needles, cast on 13 sts and starting with a K row work in st st for 15cm, ending with a K row. Slip all sts onto a stitch holder.

LEFT FRONT:
Using yarn doubled throughout and 12mm needles, cast on 18(22:26)sts and work 8 rows in K1,P1 rib, ending with a WS row.

Change to 15mm needles and starting with a K row, work in st st until work measures 32cm, ending with a WS row.

Next row: K4(6,8) (P1,K1) five times, P1, K to end.

Next row: P3(5,7) (K1,P1) five times, K1, P to end.

Next row: K4(6,8), cast off 11sts, K to end. 7(11,15) sts.

Place pocket:
Next row (WS): P2(4,6)sts, and with WS of pocket lining facing purl together the next st along with the first st of the pocket lining, purl across pocket lining until 1 st remains on stitch holder, purl together this st with next stitch on main body of work, purl to end. 18(22,26)sts

Cont straight in st st until work measures 92(94,96)cm, ending with a RS row.

SHAPE NECK:
Cast off 3sts and pattern to end. 15[19, 23]sts.
Decrease 1 st at neck edge on next 2 alt rows. 13[17, 21]sts.
Cont straight until work matches back. Cast off.

RIGHT FRONT:
Work as left front, reversing all shapings and pocket placement.

SLEEVES (Make two):
Using yarn doubles and 12mm needels, cast on 16(18,20)sts and work 10 rows in K1, P1 rib.

Change to 15mm needels and starting with a K row, work in st st, inc 1 st at each end of 5ᵗʰ and every foll 4ᵗʰ row until 34(36:38)sts.
Cont straight until work measures 47(49:49)cm, ending with a WS row.
Cast off.

FINISHING:
Join shoulder seams.

LEFT FRONT BAND:
Using yarn doubles and 12mm needles, with RS facing and starting at the top left front edge, pick up and knit 75(77:79)sts down left front edge.
Knit 1 row.
Cast off loosely.

RIGHT FRONT BAND:
Work as for left front band, starting at the base of the right front edge.

NECK:
Using yarn doubled and 12mm needles, with RS facing and starting at top of the right front band, pick up and knit, 14sts along right side of neck, 4sts across to back neck sts held on stitch holder, 12sts from stitch holder at back neck, 4sts across to left front, 14sts down left neck shaping. [48]sts.

Knit 1 row.

Cast off loosely.

Sew in sleeves.
Join side and sleeve seams.
Sew pocket seams.

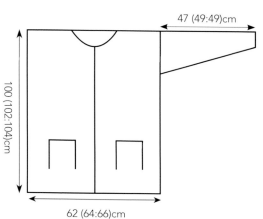

47 (49:49)cm

100 (102:104)cm

62 (64:66)cm

Ellie

SIZES: XS (S, M, L, XL, XXL)

YARN USAGE: 9 (9, 10, 10, 11, 12) balls of Rowan Summerlite 4ply (shown in shade 422)

NEEDLES: 3mm (3US) and 3.25mm (3US), 3mm/80cm circular needle

EXTRAS: Stitch holder

TENSION: 28sts and 36rows = 10cm measured over st st using 3.25mm needles.

RIB PATTERN:
Row 1: *P3, K1 rep from * to last 2 sts p2.
Row 2: K2, *P1, K3 rep from * to end.

BACK:
Using 3mm needles, cast on 126(134,142,154,166,182)sts and work in rib pattern for 8cm, ending with a WS row.

Change to 3.25mm needles and starting with a K row, work in st st until work measures 55(55,56,56,56,56)cm, ending with a WS row.

SHAPE ARMHOLE:
Cast off 6sts at the beg of next 2 rows. 114[122, 130, 142, 154, 170]sts.

Dec 1 st at each end of next and foll 6 alt rows. 100[108, 116, 128, 140, 156]sts

Cont straight until armhole measures 20(21,21,22,23,24)cm, ending with a WS row.

SHAPE BACK NECK:
Patt 25(29, 33, 39, 45, 53)sts, turn.
P2tog, work to end. 24[28, 32, 38, 44, 52]sts.
Cast off.
Slip centre 50sts onto a stitch holder and work other side to match.

LEFT FRONT:

Using 3mm needles, cast on 58(62,66,70,78,86)sts and work in rib pattern for 8cm, ending with a WS row.

Change to 3.25mm needles and starting with a K row, work in st st until work measures 14 rows less than before armhole shaping of back, ending with a RS row.

SHAPE NECK:

Dec 1 st at neck edge on next and every following 4th row.
AT THE SAME TIME, when work measures 55(55,56,56,56,56)cm, beg with a RS row, shape armhole.

SHAPE ARMHOLE:

Cast off 6sts at beg of next row.

Purl 1 row.

Dec 1 st at armhole edge of next and 6 following alt rows.

Dec on front slope as set until 24(28, 32, 38, 44, 52)sts. Work straight until work measures same as back, ending with a WS row.
Cast off.

RIGHT FRONT:

Work as left front, reversing all shapings.

SLEEVES (make two):

Using 3mm needles, cast on 58(58,58,62,66,66)sts and work 4cm in rib pattern, ending with a WS row. Change to 3.25mm needles and starting with a K row work in st st, inc 1 st at each end of 5th and every foll 4th row until 116(116,116, 120,120,124)sts. Cont straight until work measures 47(48,48,49,50,51)cm ending with a WS row.

SHAPE SLEEVE TOP:

Cast off 6sts at beg of next 2 rows. 104[104,104,108,108,112]sts.

Dec 1 st at each end of next and foll 6 alt rows. 90[90,90,94,94,98]sts.
Work 1 row.
Cast off.

FINISHING:

Join shoulder seams.

FRONT AND NECK BANDS:

Using a 3mm/80cm circular needle, with RS facing and starting at the lower edge of right front, pick up and knit 98(100,102,104,106,106sts along right front edge, 56sts up right front neck shaping, 3sts across back, 50sts from back stitch holder, 3sts back neck to shoulder seam, 56sts down right neck shaping, 98(100,102,104,106,106)sts down left front. 364[368, 372, 376, 380, 380]sts.

Row 1(WS): K3,P1 to end.
Work in rib as set for 5 rows, ending with a WS row.
Starting with a K row, work 4 rows in st st.
Cast off loosely.
Sew in sleeves.
Join side and sleeve seams.

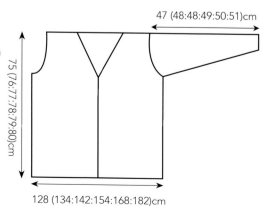

47 (48:48:49:50:51)cm

75 (76:77:78:79:80)cm

128 (134:142:154:168:182)cm

Abbreviations

K – knit

P – purl

st(s) – stitch(es)

inc – increas(e)(ing)

dec – decreas(e)(ing)

st st – stocking stitch (1 row knit, 1 row purl)

g st – garter stitch (every row knit)

beg – begin(ning)

foll – following

rem – remain(ing)

alt – alternate

cont – continue

patt – pattern

tog – together

mm – millimetres

cm – centimetres

in – inch(es)

RS – right side

WS – wrong side

sl 1 – slip one stitch

psso – pass slipped stitch over

p2sso – pass 2 slipped stitches over

tbl – through back of loop

m1 – make one stitch by picking up loop between last and next stitch and working into the back of this loop

yfwd - bring yarn forward between the needles and then back over before making the next stitch. 1 st inc'd.

meas – measures

wyif – with yarn in front

wyib – with yarn at back

pm – place marker

ROWAN STOCKISTS

AUSTRALIA: Australian Country Spinners, Pty Ltd, Level 7, 409 St. Kilda Road, Melbourne Vic 3004.
Tel: 03 9380 3888 Fax: 03 9820 0989
email: customerservice@auspinners.com.au

AUSTRIA:: MEZ Harlander GmbH, Schulhof 6, 1. Stock, 1010 Wien, Austria
Tel: + 00800 26 27 28 00 Fax: (00) 49 7644 802-133 Email: verkauf.harlander@mezcrafts.com Web: www.mezcrafts.at

BELGIUM: MEZ crafts Belgium NV, c/o MEZ GmbH, Kaiserstr.1, 79341 Kenzingen Germany Tel: 0032 (0) 800 77 89 2
Fax: 00 49 7644 802 133 Email: sales.be-nl@mezcrafts.com
Web: www.mezcrafts.be

BULGARIA: MEZ Crafts Bulgaria EOOD, Bul. Rozhen 25A, BG-1220 Sofia, Bulgaria Tel: +359 2 439 24 24 Fax: +359 2 439 24 28
Email: office.bg@mezcrafts.com

CHINA: Commercial agent Mr Victor Li, c/o MEZ GmbH Germany, Kaiserstr. 1, 79341 Kenzingen / Germany
Tel: (86- 21) 13816681825 Email: victor.li@mezcrafts.com

CHINA: SHANGHAI YUJUN CO.,LTD, Room 701 Wangjiao Plaza, No.175 Yan'an(E), 200002 Shanghai, China
Tel: +86 2163739785 Email: jessechang@vip.163.com

CYPRUS: MEZ Crafts Bulgaria EOOD, Bul. Rozhen 25A, BG-1220 Sofia, Bulgaria Tel: +359 2 439 24 24 Fax: +359 2 439 24 28
Email: office.bg@mezcrafts.com

CZECH REPUBLIC: Coats Czecho s.r.o. Staré Mesto 246 569-32
Tel: (420) 461616633 Email: galanterie@coats.com

DENMARK: Carl J. Permin A/S Egegaardsvej 28 DK-2610 Rødovre
Tel: (45) 36 72 12 00 E-mail: permin@permin.dk

ESTONIA: MEZ Crafts Estonia OÜ, Ampri tee 9/4, 74001 Viimsi Harjumaa
Tel: +372 630 6252 Email: info.ee@mezcrafts.com
Web: www.coatscrafts.co.ee

FINLAND: MEZ Crafts Finland Oy, Huhtimontie 6, 04200 Kerava
Tel: (358) 9 274 871 Email: sales.fi@mezcrafts.com
www.coatscrafts.fi

FRANCE: 3bcom, 35 avenue de Larrieu, 31094 Toulouse cedex 01, France
Tel: 0033 (0) 562 202 096 Email: Commercial@3b-com.com

GERMANY: MEZ GmbH, Kaiserstr. 1, 79341 Kenzingen, Germany
Tel: 0049 7644 802 222 Email: kenzingen.vertrieb@mezcrafts.com Fax: 0049 7644 802 300
Web: www.mezcrafts.de

GREECE: MEZ Crafts Bulgaria EOOD, Bul. Rozhen 25A, BG-1220 Sofia, Bulgaria Tel: +359 2 439 24 24 Fax: +359 2 439 24 28 Email: office.bg@mezcrafts.com

HOLLAND: G. Brouwer & Zn B.V., Oudhuijzerweg 69, 3648 AB Wilnis, Netherlands Tel: 0031 (0) 297-281 557
Email: info@gbrouwer.nl

HONG KONG: East Unity Company Ltd, Unit B2, 7/F., Block B, Kailey Industrial Centre, 12 Fung Yip Street, Chai Wan
Tel: (852)2869 7110 Email: eastunityco@yahoo.com.hk

ICELAND: Carl J. Permin A/S Egegaardsvej 28 DK-2610 Rødovre
Tel: (45) 36 72 12 00 Email: permin@permin.dk

ITALY: Mez Cucirini Italy Srl, Viale Sarca, 223, 20126 MILANO
Tel.: 02 636151 Fax: 02 66111701

JAPAN: Hobbyra Hobbyre Corporation, 23-37, 5-Chome, Higashi-Ohi, Shinagawa-Ku, 1400011 Tokyo. Tel +81334721104
Daidoh International, 3-8-11 Kudanminami Chiyodaku, Hiei Kudan Bldg 5F, 1018619 Tokyo. Tel +81-3-3222-7076 Fax +81-3-3222-7066

KOREA: My Knit Studio, 3F, 144 Gwanhun-Dong, 110-300 Jongno-Gu, Seoul
Tel: 82-2-722-0006 Email: myknit@myknit.com Web: www.myknit.com

LATVIA: Coats Latvija SIA, Mukusalas str. 41 b, Riga LV-1004
Tel: +371 67 625173 Fax: +371 67 892758 Email: info.latvia@coats.com
Web: www.coatscrafts.lv

LEBANON: y.knot, Saifi Village, Mkhalissiya Street 162, Beirut
Tel: (961) 1 992211 Fax: (961) 1 315553 Email: y.knot@cyberia.net.lb

LITHUANIA & RUSSIA: MEZ Crafts Lithuania UAB, A. Juozapaviciaus str: 6/2, LT-09310 Vilnius Tel: +370 527 30971 Fax: +370 527 2305 Email: info.lt@mezcrafts.com Web: www.coatscrafts.lt

LUXEMBOURG: Coats N.V., c/o Coats GmbH, Kaiserstr. 1, 79341 Kenzingen, Germany Tel: 00 49 7644 802 222 Fax: 00 49 7644 802 133
Email: sales.coatsninove@coats.com Web: www.coatscrafts.be

MEXICO: Estambres Crochet SA de CV, Aaron Saenz 1891-7Pte, 64650 MONTERREY TEL +52 (81) 8335-3870
Email: abremer@redmundial.com.mx

NEW ZEALAND: ACS New Zealand, P.O. Box 76199, Northwood, Christchurch, New Zealand Tel: 64 3 323 6665 Fax: 64 3 323 6660
Email: lynn@impactmg.co.nz

NORWAY: Carl J. Permin A/S Egegaardsvej 28 DK-2610 Rødovre
Tel: (45) 36 72 12 00 E-mail: permin@permin.dk

PORTUGAL: Mez Crafts Portugal, Lda – Av. Vasco da Gama, 774 - 4431-059 V.N, Gaia, Portugal Tel: 00 351 223 770700 Email: sales.iberia@mezcrafts.com

SINGAPORE: Golden Dragon Store, BLK 203 Henderson Rd #07-02, 159546 Henderson Indurstrial Park Singapore
Tel: (65) 62753517 Fax: (65) 62767112 Email: gdscraft@hotmail.com

SLOVAKIA: MEZ Crafts Slovakia, s.r.o. Seberíniho 1, 821 03 Bratislava, Slovakia Tel: +421 2 32 30 31 19 Email: galanteria@mezcrafts.com

SOUTH AFRICA: Arthur Bales LTD, 62 4th Avenue, Linden 2195
Tel: (27) 11 888 2401 Fax: (27) 11 782 6137 Email: arthurb@new.co.za
Web: www.arthurbales.co.za

SPAIN: MEZ Fabra Spain S.A, Avda Meridiana 350, pta 13 D, 08027 Barcelona Tel: +34 932908400 Fax: +34 932908409 Email: atencion.clientes@mezcrafts.com

SWEDEN: Carl J. Permin A/S Egegaardsvej 28 DK-2610 Rødovre
Tel: (45) 36 72 12 00 E-mail: permin@permin.dk

SWITZERLAND: MEZ Crafts Switzerland GmbH, Stroppelstrasse20, 5417 Untersiggenthal, Switzerland Tel: +41 00800 2627 2800 Fax: 0049 7644 802 133 Email: verkauf.ch@mezcrafts.com
Web: www.mezcrafts.ch

TURKEY: MEZ Crafts Tekstil A.□, Kavacık Mahallesi, Ekinciler Cad. Necip Fazıl Sok. No.8 Kat: 5, 34810 Beykoz / Istanbul
Tel: +90 216 425 88 10 www.mezcrafts.com

TAIWAN: Cactus Quality Co Ltd, 7FL-2, No. 140, Sec.2 Roosevelt Rd, Taipei, 10084 Taiwan, R.O.C. Tel: 00886-2-23656527 Fax: 886-2-23656503
Email: cqcl@ms17.hinet.net

THAILAND: Global Wide Trading, 10 Lad Prao Soi 88, Bangkok 10310
Tel: 00 662 933 9019 Fax: 00 662 933 9110
Email: global.wide@yahoo.com

U.K: Mez Craft UK Ltd, 17F Brooke's Mill, Armitage Bridge Huddersfield, HD4 7NR Tel: +44 (0) 1484 768878 Fax: +44 (0) 1484 690 838
Web: www.knitrowan.com

Information

TENSION

This is the size of your knitting. Most of the knitting patterns will have a tension quoted. This is how many stitches 10cm/4in in width and how many rows 10cm/4in in length to make a square. If your knitting doesn't match this then your finished garment will not measure the correct size. To obtain the correct measurements for your garment you must achieve the tension.

The tension quoted on a ball band is the manufacturer's average. For the manufacturer and designers to produce designs they have to use a tension for you to be able to obtain the measurements quoted. It's fine not to be the average, but you need to know if you meet the average or not. Then you can make the necessary adjustments to obtain the correct measurements.

CHOOSING YARN

Choosing yarn, as one of my friends once described "It is like shopping in an adult's sweetie shop". I think this sums it up very well. All the colours and textures, where do you start? Look for the thickness, how chunky do you want your finished garment? Sometimes it's colour that draws you to a yarn or perhaps you have a pattern that requires a specific yarn. Check the washing/care instructions before you buy.

Yarn varies in thickness; there are various descriptions such as DK and 4ply these are examples of standard weights. There are a lot of yarns available that are not standard and it helps to read the ball band to see what the recommended needle size is.

This will give you an idea of the approximate thickness. It is best to use the yarn recommended in the pattern.

Keep one ball band from each project so that you have a record of what you have used and most importantly how to care for your garment after it has been completed. Always remember to give the ball band with the garment if it is a gift.

The ball band normally provides you with the average tension and recommended needle sizes for the yarn, this may vary from what has been used in the pattern, always go with the pattern as the designer may change needles to obtain a certain look. The ball band also tells you the name of the yarn and what it is made of, the weight and approximate length of the ball of yarn along with the shade and dye lot numbers. This is important as dye lots can vary, you need to buy your yarn with matching dye lots.

PRESSING AND AFTERCARE

Having spent so long knitting your project it can be a great shame not to look after it properly. Some yarns are suitable for pressing once you have finished to improve the look of the fabric. To find out this information you will need to look on the yarn ball band, where there will be washing and care symbols.

Once you have checked to see if your yarn is suitable to be pressed and the knitting is a smooth texture (stocking stitch for example), pin out and place a damp cloth onto the knitted pieces. Hold the steam iron (at the correct temperature) approximately 10cm/4in away from the fabric and steam. Keep the knitted pieces pinned in place until cool.

As a test it is a good idea to wash your tension square in the way you would expect to wash your garment.

WITH THANKS

q u a i l   s t u d i o would like to thank Jesse Wild for his amazing photography, and our design team for their work on this project. To our dedicated team of knitters who worked around the clock to turn the projects around, and Hollie from BMA for her modeling skills and paitence. Then finally David and the team at Rowan for their support on this project and yarn sponsorship.